simple gifts for dog love

simple gifts for dog lovers

CATHERINE TOUGH

PHOTOGRAPHY BY JOHN HESELTINE

Martingale®
& COMPANY

First published in 2007 by Coats Crafts UK,
Lingfield Point, McMullen Road,
Darlington DL1 1YQ, UK

First published in the USA in 2008 by
Martingale & Company ®
20205 144th Ave. NE
Woodinville, WA 98072-8478 USA
www.martingale-pub.com

Martingale
& C O M P A N Y

Reproduced and printed in Singapore
13 12 11 10 09 08   6 5 4 3 2 1

Copyright © 2007 Coats Crafts UK
Photography copyright © John Heseltine
Design copyright © Catherine Tough
Illustrations copyright © Ed Berry

Editor Susan Berry
Designer Anne Wilson
Illustrations Ed Berry
Technician Penny Hill

Library of Congress Cataloging-in-Publication
Data is available.

ISBN-13: 978-1-56477-871-0

contents

introduction

Dogs make much loved pets, so why not demonstrate your affection by making something special either for your own dog or for a friend's?

The designs in this book are simple and inexpensive to create, and most involve only the most basic craft skills in knitting, crochet, or stitching.

I have included a range of different projects, from a little coat and scarf for a dog to wear to some dog-inspired gifts for owners, too, such as a bone-shaped key fob and an embroidered picture frame for a favorite dog portrait.

Whatever you make as a gift, take the time and trouble to present it well—wrap it up with an extra-special paper, then cut out a little bone shape from stiff paper for a special gift tag and tie it on with a colorful wool yarn!

projects

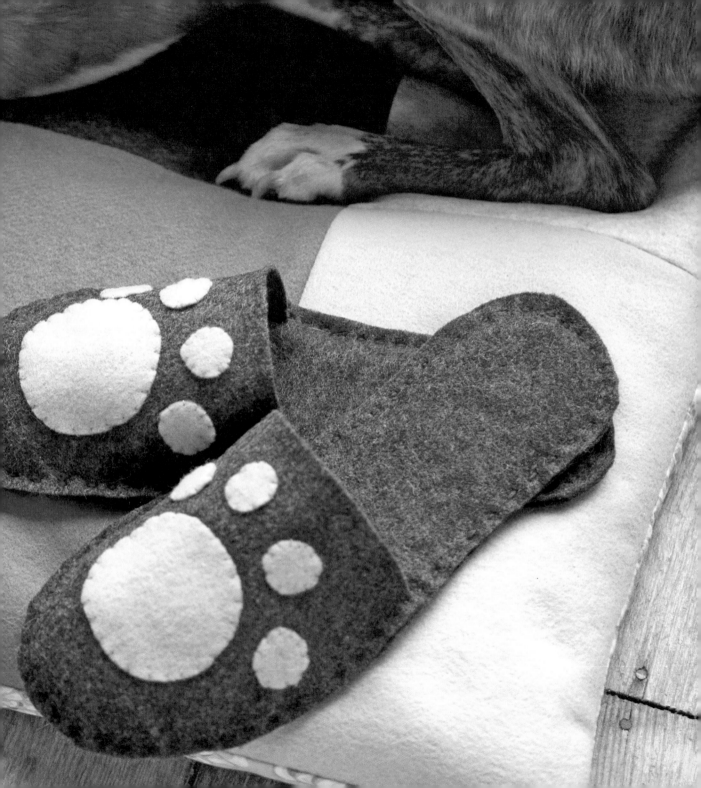

dog coat

Your dog will look cute and stay warm in this hand-knitted stripy coat. Knitted in stockinette stitch with ribbed edgings, cuffs, and collar, it slips easily over the dog's head.

The coat is designed to fit a small to medium-size dog and comes in two colorways: one for him and one for her. If you want a high-necked version, knit the turtleneck variation.

Make the little dog scarf on page 14 to complete the outfit.

MEASUREMENTS

Approximately 12in (30cm) long by 19¾in (50cm) in circumference.

MATERIALS

A DK-weight wool-mix yarn  each 1¾oz (50g) ball is approximately 131yd (120m) long—*see page 64*

Male dog

1 ball each in mid denim blue (**MC**), dark navy blue (**A**), beige (**B**), and dark gray (**C**)

Pair each of sizes 5 and 6 (3.75mm and 4mm) knitting needles

Size 5 (3.75mm) circular needle

Female dog

1 ball each in apple green (**MC**), hot pink (**A**), pale pink (**B**), and dark thyme green (**C**)

Pair each of sizes 5 and 6 (3.75mm and 4mm) knitting needles

Size 5 (3.75mm) circular needle

GAUGE

22 sts and 30 rows to 4in (10cm) over St st using size 6 (4mm) needles *or size necessary to obtain correct gauge.*

ABBREVIATIONS

See page 58.

SPECIAL NOTE

Cast on the stitches for the upper body and under body loosely.

TO MAKE COAT

Upper body

With size 5 (3.75mm) needles and A, cast on 66 sts.

Rib row 1 (RS) K4, *P2, K2; rep from * to last 6 sts, P2, K4.

Rib row 2 K2, *P2, K2; rep from * to end.

Rep the last 2 rows 7 times more.

Cut off A.

Change to size 6 (4mm) needles and join B.

Next row (RS) K to end.

Next row K2, P to last 2 sts, K2.

Rep the last 2 rows 7 times more.

Cut off B.

Join MC.

Mark each end of last row with a colored thread.

Next row (RS) K to end.

Next row P to end.

Rep the last 2 rows 7 times more.

Cut off MC.

Join C.

Next row (RS) K to end.

Next row P to end.

Rep the last 2 rows 7 times more.

Cut off C.

Join MC.

Cont in St st until work measures 12in (29cm) from cast-on edge, ending with a P row.

Mark each end of last row with a colored thread to mark top of leg opening.

Bind off one st at beg of next 2 rows. *64 sts.*

Leave these sts on a spare needle.

Under body

With size 5 (3.75mm) needles and MC, cast on 48 sts.

Rib row 1 K3, *P2, K2; rep from * to last 5 sts, P2, K3.

Rib row 2 P3, *K2, P2; rep from * to last 5 sts, K2, P3.

Rep the last 2 rows until work measures the same as upper body between colored threads.

Bind off one st at beg of next 2 rows. *46 sts.*

Leave these sts on a spare needle.

Front leg bands

Leaving 3½in (9cm) open at top for leg opening, join under body to upper body, matching cast-on edge of under body to first colored thread on upper body.

With RS facing and using size 5 (3.75mm) needles and A, pick up and knit 42 sts evenly along open edges, starting and stopping at marker near top edge.

Rib row 1 (WS) K2, *P2, K2; rep from * to end.

Rib row 2 P2, *K2, P2; rep from * to end.

Rep the last 2 rows 4 times more.

Bind off in rib.

Collar

With RS of coat facing and using size 5 (3.75mm) circular needle and A, rib across 46 sts on under body, then across upper-body stitches K2, *skp, K2tog, K1; rep from * ending last rep K3. *86 sts.*

Rib row 1 (RS of collar) P2, *K2, P2; rep from * to end.

Rib row 2 K2, *P2, K2; rep from * to end.

Rep the last 2 rows 8 times more and the first row again.

Turtleneck variation:

Rep the last 2 rows 16 times more and the first row again.

Both versions:

Bind off in rib.

Finishing

Sew right leg seam. Sew left leg seam and collar seam.

dog and owner scarves

Here are two versions of a simple stripy scarf in garter stitch: one for your dog and one for you. You can opt for whichever colorway you prefer.

The owner's scarf is backed with a matching printed fabric (so that the ends of each newly joined color are neatly hidden under the fabric) and fringed with one of the contrasting colors. For the little dog scarf, it is easier to weave in the ends (see page 56), but you could back it with fabric, if you prefer.

MEASUREMENTS

Dog scarf: 2¼in (6cm) wide by 10¼in (23cm) long.
Owner scarf: 4½in (12cm) wide by 45in (115cm) long.

MATERIALS

A DK-weight wool-mix yarn **3 LIGHT** each 1¾oz (50g) ball is approximately 131yd (120m) long—*see page 64*
Dog scarf: 1 ball each in apple green (**A**), mid denim blue (**B**), light delphinium blue (**C**), beige (**D**), and turquoise (**E**)
Owner scarf: 1 ball each in honey gold (**A**), light lilac (**B**), dark lilac (**C**), beige (**D**), and taupe (**E**)

Pair of size 6 (4mm) knitting needles
Backing (optional)—8in (20cm) of printed cotton fabric, 45in (115cm) wide, and matching sewing thread

GAUGE

20 sts and 44 rows to 4in (10cm) over garter st using size 6 (4mm) needles *or size necessary to obtain correct gauge.*

ABBREVIATIONS

See page 58.

SIMPLE GIFTS FOR DOG LOVERS

TO MAKE SCARVES

Dog scarf

With size 6 (4mm) needles and A, cast on 12 sts.
Work in garter st (knit every row) and stripes as follows:
4 rows B, 2 rows C, 5 rows B, 1 row D, 3 rows E,
5 rows C, 2 rows D, 6 rows B, 2 rows C, 1 row A,
3 rows B, 2 rows E, 6 rows C, 1 row D, 2 rows E,
6 rows B, 1 row A, 5 rows C, 4 rows B, 1 row A.
Rep this 62-row stripe patt until scarf measures 24in
(60cm) from cast-on edge.
Bind off. Weave in loose ends (see page 56).

Owner scarf

With size 6 (4mm) needles and A, cast on 24 sts.
Cont in garter st (knit every row) and stripes as follows:
4 rows B, 2 rows C, 5 rows B, 1 row D, 3 rows E,
5 rows C, 2 rows D, 6 rows C, 2 rows B, 1 row A,
3 rows B, 2 rows E, 6 rows C, 1 row D, 2 rows E,
6 rows B, 1 row A, 5 rows C, 4 rows B, 1 row A.
Rep this 62-row stripe patt until scarf measures 45in
(115cm) from cast-on edge, ending with 1 row A.
Using A, bind off.

Backing for owner scarf (optional)

Cut backing fabric to same size as scarf plus a seam
allowance all around the edge. Fold and press seam
allowance to wrong side along raw edges of backing
fabric so that backing is same size as scarf.
With wrong sides together, baste backing to scarf, then
sew in place. Remove basting.

Fringe for owner scarf

Cut 48 lengths of yarn A, each 10in (25cm) long. Fold
two lengths (held together) in half and knot into every
alternate stitch along scarf ends to form fringe.

dog blanket

This patchwork dog blanket is very easy to knit and sew; in fact, it is so simple that even if you are an absolute beginner you could still make it very successfully.

The blanket is made up of rectangles in plain and striped garter stitch and in printed fabric (backed with felt), patched together as shown.

The yarns and fabrics used are all washable— an essential prerequisite of any dog blanket.

MEASUREMENTS

Approximately 27½in (70cm) wide by 40in (100cm) long.

MATERIALS

An Aran-weight wool-mix yarn  each 1¾oz (50g)
  ball is approximately 78yd (74m) long—*see page 64*

3 balls in red (**A**)

2 balls each in silver (**B**) and russet (**C**)

1 ball each in orange (**D**), gold (**E**), chartreuse (**F**),
  lavender (**G**), and gray (**H**)

Pair of size 9 (5.5mm) knitting needles

Piece of red felt 10¾in (27cm) by 13¼in (33cm)

Piece of ruby felt 7¾in (20cm) by 13¼in (33cm)

Piece of orange felt 6in (15cm) by 13½in (34cm)

13¾in (35cm) of printed cotton fabric, 45in (115cm)
  wide, and matching sewing thread

GAUGE

15 sts and 34 rows to 4in (10cm) over garter st using
size 9 (5.5mm) needles *or size necessary to obtain
correct gauge.*

ABBREVIATIONS

See page 58.

SPECIAL NOTE

First row in garter st on knitted patches is a WS row.

TO MAKE BLANKET

Patch A

With size 9 (5.5mm) needles and E, cast on 50 sts.
Work 3 rows in garter st (knit every row).
Cont in garter st throughout, work 4 rows D, 4 rows A,
and 4 rows E.
Rep last 12 rows until patch measures 11¾in (30cm)
from cast-on edge, ending with a WS row. Bind off.

Patch B

Cut a piece of red felt 10¾in (27cm) by 13¼in (33cm)
(see page 64).
Cut a piece of fabric 11¾in (30cm) by 14¼in (36cm),
fold and press ½in (1.5cm) to wrong side all around
outer edge, then topstitch to red felt of same size.

Patch C

With size 9 (5.5mm) needles and B, cast on 50 sts.
Work in garter st (knit every row) until patch measures 5in
(13cm) from cast-on edge, ending with a WS row. Bind off.

Patch D

Cut a piece of ruby felt 7¾in (20cm) by 13¼in (33cm).
Cut a piece of fabric 8¾in (23cm) by 14¼in (36cm), fold

SIMPLE GIFTS FOR DOG LOVERS

and press ½in (1.5cm) to wrong side all around outer edge, then topstitch to ruby felt of same size.

Patch E

With size 9 (5.5mm) needles and F, cast on 50 sts.
Work in garter st until patch measures 5in (13cm) from cast-on edge, ending with a WS row.
Using G, cont in garter st until patch measures 9¾in (25cm) from cast-on edge, ending with a WS row.
Using C, cont in garter st until patch measures 19¾in (50cm) from cast-on edge, ending with a WS row. Bind off.

Patch F

With size 9 (5.5mm) needles and A, cast on 51 sts.
Work in garter st until patch measures 11¾in (30cm) from cast-on edge, ending with a WS row. Bind off.

Patch G

Cut a piece of orange felt 6in (15cm) by 13½in (34cm).
Cut a piece of fabric 7in (18cm) by 14½in (37cm), fold and press ½in (1.5cm) to wrong side all around outer edge, then topstitch to orange felt of same size.

Patch H

With size 9 (5.5mm) needles and H, cast on 51 sts.
Work 3 rows in garter st.
Cont in garter st throughout, work 4 rows B and 4 rows H.
Rep last 8 rows until patch measures 9¾in (25cm) from cast-on edge, ending with a WS row. Bind off.

Finishing

Using overcast stitches, sew patches together as shown on opposite page—with patches A, B, and C in bottom horizontal row, D and E in center horizontal row, and F, G, and H in top horizontal row.

knitted dog bed

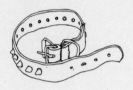

This project is simple enough for a novice knitter, because all you have to knit are six simple rectangles in stockinette stitch and then sew them together, alternating the knit and purl sides of the fabric. To finish off, you add backing fabric and some batting.

If you don't feel like taking the time to do the knitting, make a similar dog bed in felt (see pages 26–29).

MEASUREMENTS

Approximately 24in (60cm) wide by 39½in (100cm) long.

MATERIALS

An Aran-weight wool-mix yarn **4 MEDIUM** each 1¾oz (50g)
 ball is approximately 78yd (74m) long—*see page 64*
2 balls each in charcoal (**A**), silver (**B**), navy (**C**), teal (**D**),
 beige (**E**), and lavender (**F**)
Pair of size 9 (5.5mm) knitting needles
51in (130cm) of printed cotton fabric, 45in (115cm) wide,
 and matching sewing thread
Thick batting 24in (60cm) by 39½in (100cm)

GAUGE

16.5 sts and 22 rows to 4in (10cm) over St st using size 9
(5.5mm) needles *or size necessary to obtain correct gauge.*

ABBREVIATIONS

See page 58.

TO MAKE BED

Knitted rectangles (make 6)

With size 9 (5.5mm) needles and A, cast on 55 sts.
Beg with a knit row, work 66 rows in St st. Bind off.
Work 5 more rectangles in same way, but using a
different color for each (B, C, D, E, and F).

Preparing top

Sew knitted rectangles together (see page 56),
alternating knit and purl sides of fabric (as shown on
opposite page), to form top of bed.

Preparing backing

Cut fabric in half crosswise to make two pieces 25½in
(65cm) by 45in (115cm).
Make a hem along one short side on each backing
piece: fold and press ¾in (2cm) then 2in (5cm) to wrong
side, and stitch hem in place. Lap one piece of backing

over the other by 10in (25cm) and baste pieces together along overlapping sections (see page 63).

Fold a seam allowance to wrong side all around outer edge of backing so that the backing is same size as knitted top; trim off excess fabric.

Finishing

With wrong sides together, baste knitted top to backing.

Topstitch backing in place and remove basting.

Insert batting through envelope back.

felt dog bed

This is a patchwork felt version of the knitted dog bed shown on page 22. It is made similarly, with a top, backing, and batting insert.

If you want to make a larger bed, you could add a third row of patchwork rectangles, in the same color combinations as the first row, and increase the size of the backing and batting accordingly.

MEASUREMENTS

Approximately 21½in (56cm) by 33¾in (85cm).

MATERIALS

2 pieces of felt, each 11¾in (30cm) by 7¾in (19cm),
   in each of five colors: lavender, pale gray, charcoal,
   chocolate, and sandstone
51in (130cm) of printed cotton fabric, 45in (115cm)
   wide, and matching sewing thread
Thick batting 23½in (60cm) by 35½in (90cm)

TIP

Make sure you cut each felt piece to exactly the same
size and take the same seam allowance to ensure that
the seams match exactly.

TO MAKE BED

Top

Cut two pieces of felt, each 11¾in (30cm) by 7¾in
(19cm), from each of the five colors of felt.
Taking ½in (1cm) seams, stitch five felt pieces together
in each vertical row as shown, to form two long strips.
Carefully matching the seams, stitch the two strips
together to create the rectangular top.

Backing

Cut fabric in half crosswise to make two pieces each
25½in (65cm) by 45in (115cm).
Make a hem along one short side on each piece: first
fold and press ¾in (2cm), then 2in (5cm) to wrong side,
and then stitch hem in place.
Lap one backing piece over the other by 10in (25cm)
and baste in place (see page 63).
Cut backing to the same size as top.

Finishing

With right sides together, baste top to backing; then
stitch together ½in (1cm) from edge.
Remove basting, turn right side out, and insert the
batting in the bed.

key fob

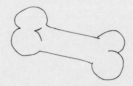

This little key fob, in the shape of a bone, makes a great gift and is very easy to sew. If you don't want to machine stitch the pieces of felt together, you could hand stitch them, using backstitch (see page 57).

Two twisted cords, each in a different colored yarn, decorate the bone shape.

MEASUREMENTS

The key fob shown here measures 6in (15cm) long.

MATERIALS

Piece of sandstone felt, 6in (15cm) square, and
   matching sewing thread
1 skein (11yd/10m) of tapestry wool needlepoint yarn
   in each of cream and orange
Small amount of rice, for filling
Special tools: funnel and metal eyelet hole-punch kit
Key ring with chain

TO MAKE KEY FOB

Preparing bone shape

Using the template as a guide, cut out two pieces of
felt. Machine stitch the two pieces together ¼in (6mm)
from the edge, leaving a small opening into which a
funnel can be inserted.

Finishing

Press the metal eyelet in place at one end of
the bone using the hole-punch kit.

A

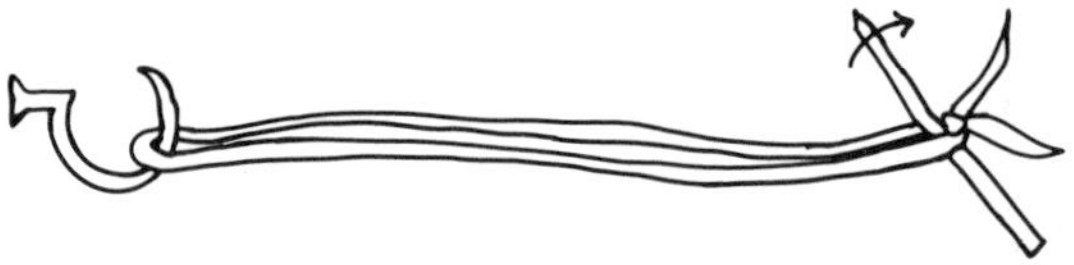

B

Using a funnel, pour in the rice filling through the
opening in the bone until it is full and firm. Stitch the
opening closed.

Make a twisted cord about 14in (36cm) long in each
yarn color. To make each cord, cut a strand 79in (210cm)
long and knot the ends together; then loop yarn onto a
handle or hook and twist using a pencil (**A**) to create a
twisted cord (**B**). Keeping taut, fold in half and allow
yarn to twist together. Then knot ends together.

Wind the cords around the bone as shown, trim if
necessary, and then sew ends in place.

Attach the key ring to the eyelet hole.

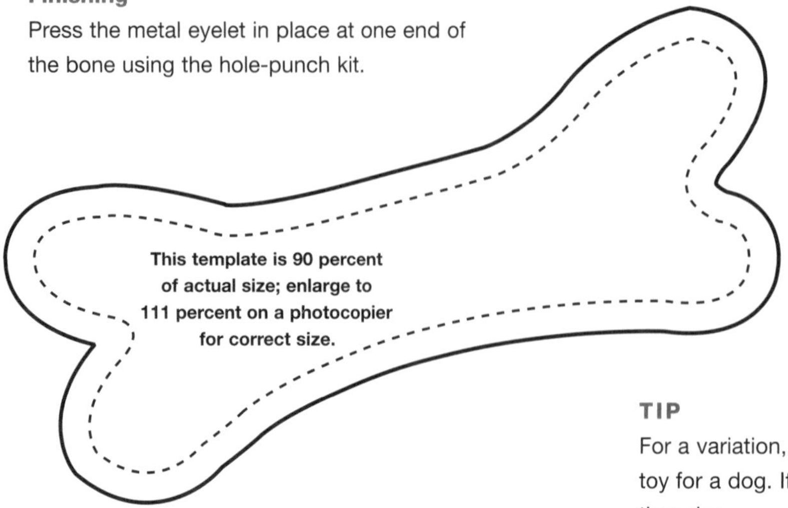

**This template is 90 percent
of actual size; enlarge to
111 percent on a photocopier
for correct size.**

TIP

For a variation, you could make a larger version as a
toy for a dog. If you do, fill the bone with fiberfill rather
than rice.

KEY FOB

grooming-kit holder

All those odds and ends—brushes, combs, scissors, and so on—that you need to ensure that your dog looks at his or her best can be kept safely in one place in this neat little roll-up grooming-kit holder.

There are his and hers versions in macho and girlie colorways, so take your pick!

The holder is made from felt and printed fabric, with little pockets to hold the various items, and is rolled up and tied with matching fabric ties. You will need a sewing machine to make this project.

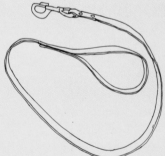

Tie

Press tie fabric in half lengthwise. Unfold and press raw edges to center fold. Turn in raw edges at ends and topstitch tie together around edges.

Finishing

Stitch center of tie to center of side edge of felt. Insert grooming items into holder, roll up, and tie.

MEASUREMENTS

Approximately 11³⁄₄in (30cm) by 17¹⁄₂in (44cm).

MATERIALS

Piece of navy or pink felt 11³⁄₄in (30cm) by 17¹⁄₂in (44cm)
12in (30cm) of printed cotton fabric, 45in (115cm) wide,
   and matching sewing thread

TO MAKE HOLDER

Cutting out

From the printed fabric, cut a piece 9in (23cm) wide by 18¹⁄₂in (47cm) long for the pocket, and a piece 1¹⁄₂in (4cm) wide by 45in (115cm) long for the tie.
Cut a piece of felt 11³⁄₄in (30cm) by 17¹⁄₂in (44cm).

Preparing printed fabric pocket

Make a hem along the top (long) edge by folding and pressing ³⁄₄in (2cm), then 1in (2.5cm) to wrong side, and stitch hem in place. Fold and press ¹⁄₂in (1.5cm) to wrong side along remaining three sides.

Sewing together felt and fabric pieces

With wrong sides together, long sides matching, and hem edge at top of pocket, baste fabric to felt. Topstitch fabric in place (see page 56).
Topstitch pocket shapes as required to fit grooming kit. Remove basting.

picture frame

A hand-embroidered picture frame with a favorite picture of a dog makes a great present. For this project, an inexpensive flat-edged frame is covered with embroidered felt. The felt is cut into four pieces to the size of the frame edge, then each one is embroidered before it is stuck to the frame.

   The embroidery stitches used here are simple to work, featuring long and short stitches in a brick pattern, but if you prefer, you could embroider the dog's name or a selection of bones and balls on the frame instead.

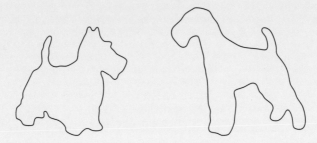

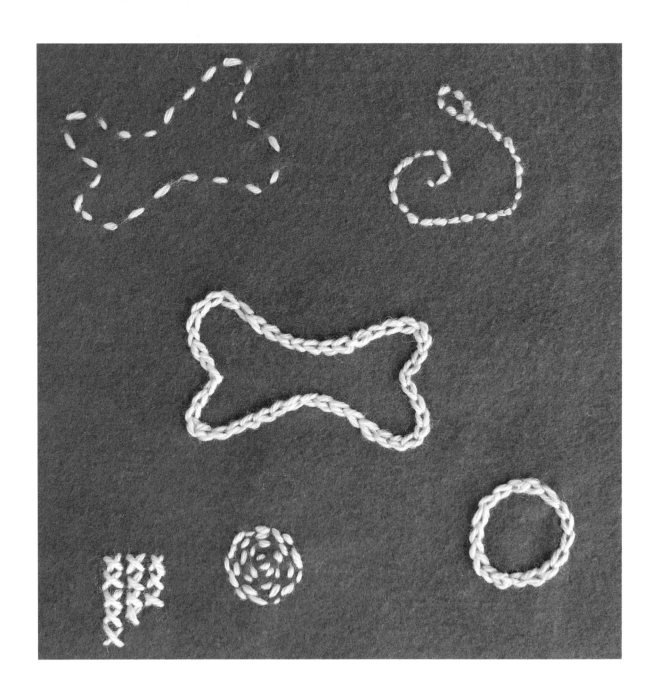

SIMPLE GIFTS FOR DOG LOVERS

MATERIALS

Rectangular flat-edged photograph frame

Enough sandstone felt to cover chosen frame

1 skein (11yd/10m) of tapestry wool needlepoint yarn
in each of 4 colors: coral, pale pink, blue, and
mid green

Large-eyed crewel embroidery needle

Double-sided tape

TO MAKE FRAME COVER

Cutting out

Measure your frame and cut the felt into four pieces, the
width of the frame border and the length measured from
the inside edge of the frame to the outer edge, as
shown in diagram: two longer pieces (**A**) and two
shorter pieces (**B**).

Embroidering

Using a ruler and pencil, mark the intended lines of
embroidery stitching on the back of each piece of felt.
With the back of the felt facing you and using the pencil
lines as a guide, embroider each felt piece in a different
color, using long and short stitches arranged so that the
long and short stitches alternate in each row to form a
brick pattern as shown (**C**).

Finishing

Stick matching pieces of double-sided
tape to the frame and to the back of the
stitched felt, and press together.
Insert photograph into frame to complete.

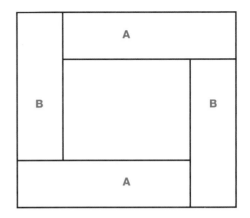

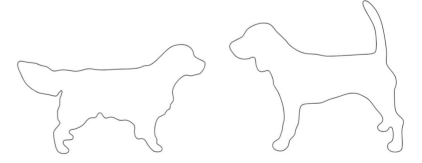

dachshund draft preventer

This cute draft preventer is made from simple knitting and a complementary printed fabric. The main body shape is made from fabric, using the knitted shape as a guide, and the knitted part is sewn on afterward.

Scaled-down in size, the dachshund would make a nice toy for a dog, too. For a toy, stuff the shape with fiberfill rather than rice.

MEASUREMENTS

Approximately 6in (15cm) wide by 31½in (80cm) long.

MATERIALS

An Aran-weight wool-mix yarn  each 1¾oz (50g) ball is approximately 78yd (74m) long—*see page 64*

2 balls in silver

Pair of size 9 (5.5mm) knitting needles

20in (50cm) of printed cotton fabric, 45in (115cm) wide, and matching sewing thread

2 buttons, for eyes

1 skein (11yd/10m) of tapestry wool needlepoint yarn in dark gray

Rice or sawdust, for filling

Special tool: funnel

GAUGE

16.5 sts and 22 rows to 4in (10cm) over St st using size 9 (5.5mm) needles *or size necessary to obtain correct gauge.*

15 sts and 34 rows to 4in (10cm) over garter st using size 9 (5.5mm) needles *or size necessary to obtain correct gauge.*

ABBREVIATIONS

See page 58.

TO MAKE DRAFT PREVENTER

Knitted body side

The body is worked starting at the tail end of the dog.

With size 9 (5.5mm) needles, cast on 5 sts.

Row 1 (RS) K to end.

Row 2 K1, P to last st, K1.

Row 3 K to last st, M1, K1.

Row 4 K1, P to last st, K1.

Rows 5 and 6 Rep rows 3 and 4. *7 sts.*

Rows 7–16 [Rep rows 1 and 2] 5 times.

Row 17 K1, M1, K to last st, M1, K1.

Row 18 K1, P to last st, K1.

Rows 19 and 20 Rep rows 17 and 18.

Row 21 K1, M1, K to last st, M1, K1. *13 sts.*

Row 22 Cast on 9 sts, K10, P to last st, K1. *22 sts.*

Row 23 K to end.

Row 24 K1, P to last st, K1.

Rows 25–134 [Rep rows 23 and 24] 55 times.

Row 135 K to end.

Row 136 K1, P to last st, M1, K1.

Row 137 K1, M1, K to end.

Rows 138 and 139 Rep rows 136 and 137.

Row 140 K1, P to last st, M1, K1. *27 sts.*

Row 141 K1, M1, K to last 3 sts, K2tog, K1.

Row 142 K1, P2tog, P to last st, M1, K1.

Row 143 K to last 3 sts, K2tog, K1.

Row 144 K1, P2tog, P to last st, M1, K1.

Row 145 K1, M1, K to last 3 sts, K2tog, K1.

Row 146 K1, P2tog, P to last st, K1. *25 sts.*

Row 147 K1, M1, K to last 3 sts, K2tog, K1.

Row 148 K1, P2tog, P to last st, K1.

Rows 149–152 [Rep rows 147 and 148] twice. *22 sts.*

Row 153 K to last 3 sts, K2tog, K1.

Row 154 K1, P2tog, P to last st, K1.

Rows 155 and 156 Rep rows 153 and 154. *18 sts.*

Row 157 K1, skp, K to last st, M1, K1.

Row 158 K1, M1, P to last 3 sts, P2tog tbl, K1.

Row 159 K to end.

Row 160 K1, M1, P to last 3 sts, P2tog tbl, K1.

Row 161 K1, skp, K to last st, M1, K1.

Row 162 K1, P to last st, K1. *18 sts.*

Row 163 K1, skp, K to last 3 sts, K2tog, K1.

Row 164 K1, P to last 3 sts, P2tog tbl, K1.

Row 165 K to end.

Row 166 K1, P2tog, P to last 3 sts, P2tog tbl, K1.

Row 167 K1, skp, K to end.

Row 168 K1, P to last st, K1. *12 sts.*

Row 169 K1, skp, K to last 3 sts, K2tog, K1.

Row 170 K1, P to last 3 sts, P2tog tbl, K1.

Rows 171–174 [Rep rows 169 and 170] twice. *3 sts.*

Row 175 K1, skp. *2 sts.*

Row 176 K2tog and fasten off.

Ears (make 2)

With size 9 (5.5mm) needles, cast on 4 sts.

K 1 row.

Next row (inc row) K1, M1, K to last st, M1, K1.

K 5 rows.

Rep the last 6 rows once more and the inc row again. *10 sts.*

K 7 rows.

Next row (dec row) K1, skp, K to last 3 sts, K2tog, K1.

K 3 rows.

Rep the last 4 rows once more. *6 sts.*

Next row K1, skp, K2tog, K1.

K 1 row.

Next row K1, skp, K1.

K 1 row.

Bind off.

Left-side legs (make 2)

With size 9 (5.5mm) needles, cast on 10 sts.

K 1 row.

Next row K1, M1, K to last 3 sts, K2tog, K1.

Next row K to end.

Rep the last 2 rows 9 times more.

Bind off.

Right-side legs (make 2)

With size 9 (5.5mm) needles, cast on 10 sts.

K 1 row.

Next row K1, skp, K to last st, M1, K1.

Next row K to end.

Rep the last 2 rows 9 times more.

Bind off.

Fabric body

Block knitted body (see page 56).

Fold fabric in half widthwise.

Using knitted piece as pattern, and allowing for a $^3/_4$in (2cm) seam, cut two body pieces from the fabric.

With right sides together, stitch pieces together, leaving an opening 4in (10cm) long. Snip seam around shaped edges. Turn right side out; then sew opening closed, leaving a small opening for funnel.

Finishing

Sew knitted side to fabric along seam line.

Using a funnel, pour in rice through opening. Sew opening closed.

Sew ears and legs in place.

Using dark gray wool embroidery yarn, embroider nose in straight stitches as shown.

Sew on buttons for eyes.

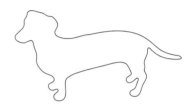

dog bag

This little carryall is just right for carrying your dog's odds and ends with you, or it could even be used as a carrier for a toy dog.

The patchwork design is a made from rectangles of plain and striped crochet mixed with patches of felt and printed fabrics, and the bag has matching fabric handles and lining.

One of the felt squares has been left plain so that you can embroider it if you wish in a simple stitch like running or chain stitch using leftover wool embroidery yarn. Work any embroidery before you stitch the pieces together.

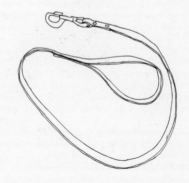

MEASUREMENTS

Approximately 11¾in (30cm) wide by 16in (40cm) deep.

MATERIALS

A DK-weight wool-mix yarn [3 LIGHT] each 1¾oz (50g)
   ball is approximately 131yd (120m) long—*see page 64*
2 balls in light gray (**A**)
1 ball each in dark gray (**B**), peacock green (**C**), coral (**D**),
   and mulberry (**E**)
Size E-4 (3.5mm) crochet hook
2 pieces of chocolate felt, each 11¾in (30cm) by 9¼in
   (23.5cm)
20in (50cm) of printed cotton fabric, 45in (115cm) wide,
   and matching sewing thread

GAUGE

20 sts and 9 rows to 4in (10cm) over double crochet
using size E-4 (3.5mm) crochet hook *or size necessary
to obtain correct gauge*.

ABBREVIATIONS

See page 58.

TO MAKE BAG

Patch A

Cut a piece of chocolate felt 7in (18cm) wide by 7¼in
(18cm) long.

Patch B

Using size E-4 (3.5mm) crochet hook and A, ch 38.
Row 1 1 dc in 4th ch from hook, 1 dc in each ch to
end, turn. *36 sts.*
Row 2 Ch 3 (to count as first dc), skip first dc, 1 dc in
each dc to end, 1 dc in 3rd ch of ch-3, turn.
Rows 3–20 [Rep row 2] 18 times. Fasten off.

Patch C

Cut a piece of printed cotton fabric 5¾in (15cm) by 5in
(13cm). Fold and press ½in (1.5cm) to wrong side all
around outer edge, and topstitch (see page 56) to felt of
same size.

Patch D

Using size E-4 (3.5mm) crochet hook and D, ch 26.
Row 1 1 dc in 4th ch from hook, 1 dc in each ch to
end, turn. *24 sts.*
Row 2 Ch 3 (to count as first dc), skip first dc, 1 dc in
each dc to end, 1 dc in 3rd of ch-3, turn.
Rows 3–9 [Rep row 2] 7 times.
Cut off D.
Join E.
Rows 10–27 [Rep row 2] 18 times.
Fasten off.

Patch E

Using size E-4 (3.5mm) crochet hook and B, ch 38.
Row 1 1 dc in 4th chain from hook, 1 dc in each ch to
end, turn. *36 sts.*
Join A.
Row 2 Using A, ch 3 (to count as first dc), skip first dc,
1 dc in each dc to end, 1 dc in 3rd of ch-3, turn.
Row 3 Using B, rep row 2.
Rows 4–35 [Rep rows 2 and 3] 16 times.
Row 36 Rep row 2.
Fasten off.

Patch F

Using size E-4 (3.5mm) crochet hook and C, ch 26.
Row 1 1 dc in 4th ch from hook, 1 dc in each ch to
end, turn. *24 sts.*
Row 2 Ch 3 (to count as first st), skip first dc, 1 dc in
each dc to end, 1 dc in 3rd of ch-3, turn.

SIMPLE GIFTS FOR DOG LOVERS

Rows 3–36 [Rep row 2] 34 times.
Fasten off.

Lining pieces
Cut two pieces of printed cotton fabric each 12¾in
(33cm) wide by 17in (43cm) long and set aside.

Handles
For two handles, cut two pieces of fabric each 11¾in
(30cm) by 2¼in (6cm). Fold and press ½in (1.5cm) to
wrong side along two long sides of each piece; then
topstitch to felt of same size.

Finishing
Overcast stitch patches A, B, C, and D together to form
one side of bag (see page 4). Overcast stitch patches E
and F together to form other side of bag (see right).
Sew both handles to inside of top edge of bag.
Make lining for bag (see page 63) and sew inside bag
with wrong sides together.

paw-print slippers

These slippers are easy to make. For a variation, you could embroider the paw-print shape on each slipper instead of using appliqué. There are some alternative shapes to stitch on page 40.

Be sure to complete any embroidery or appliqué on the upper part of the slipper before you sew it in place, remembering to leave at least $3/8$in (1cm) free all around the edge for the seams.

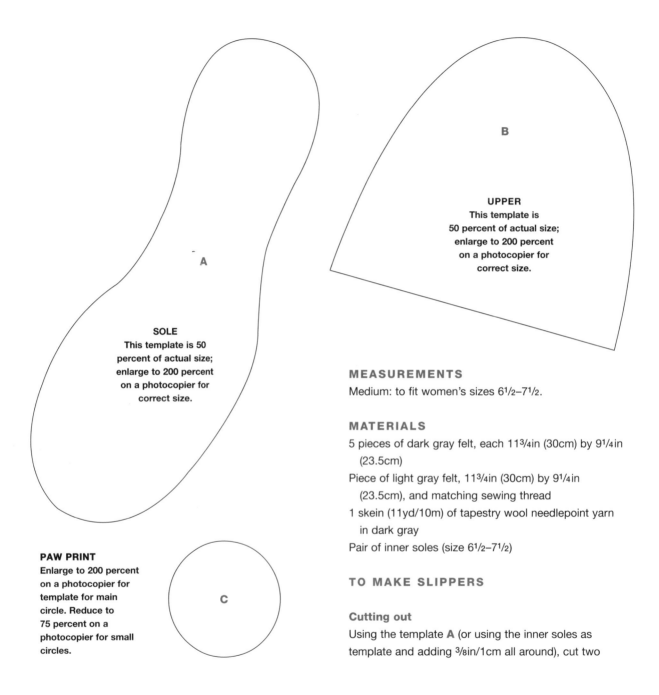

B

UPPER
This template is
50 percent of actual size;
enlarge to 200 percent
on a photocopier for
correct size.

A

SOLE
This template is 50
percent of actual size;
enlarge to 200 percent
on a photocopier for
correct size.

PAW PRINT
Enlarge to 200 percent
on a photocopier for
template for main
circle. Reduce to
75 percent on a
photocopier for small
circles.

C

MEASUREMENTS

Medium: to fit women's sizes 6½–7½.

MATERIALS

5 pieces of dark gray felt, each 11¾in (30cm) by 9¼in
(23.5cm)

Piece of light gray felt, 11¾in (30cm) by 9¼in
(23.5cm), and matching sewing thread

1 skein (11yd/10m) of tapestry wool needlepoint yarn
in dark gray

Pair of inner soles (size 6½–7½)

TO MAKE SLIPPERS

Cutting out

Using the template **A** (or using the inner soles as
template and adding ⅜in/1cm all around), cut two

pairs of soles from dark gray felt. (Each sole is a double layer of felt.) Using template **B**, cut two uppers in dark gray felt.

Using template **C**, cut one large circle and four small circles for each shoe from light gray felt.

Appliqué
Pin felt circles to each upper as shown (right) to make a paw-print shape. Then stitch in place using short straight stitches and matching thread as shown.

Seams
Easing in fullness around toes, baste each upper to one layer of felt for each slipper.

Place each inner sole between the two layers of the felt for each slipper.

Using a single strand of dark gray yarn, sew the upper to the double-layered sole, and then stitch around the back part of each sole to complete. Remove basting.

basic information

SIMPLE NEEDLEWORK TECHNIQUES

The following pages give you some help with techniques used in this book. For those who have never learned to crochet and would like to make the bag on pages 48–51, a short introduction to crochet has been included.

Basic equipment

You don't need much in the way of basic equipment to make the projects in this book. Each project gives a list of the actual materials needed, but in addition you will need a good pair of sharp scissors, blunt-ended yarn needles and ordinary sharp-pointed sewing needles, a ruler or tape measure, and an invisible marking pencil. For some of the stitched projects, it will be quicker to use a sewing machine, but you can always hand stitch the seams with backstitch (see opposite).

Before you make anything, organize all the materials and put them in a little bag or box to keep the work clean.

Knitting and crochet gauge

You need to ensure your crocheted or knitted work will turn out the right size. You do this by measuring the gauge. Your pattern will tell you how many rows and stitches are required to achieve the correct gauge.

To check that you will achieve the correct gauge, work a sample square about 5in (13cm) by 5in (13cm), using the specified stitch and knitting needle or crochet hook size. Count the number of rows and stitches across 4in (10cm) on this swatch. If these are identical to specified gauge, that is fine. But if you have more rows or stitches, use a larger needle or hook. If you have fewer rows or stitches, use a smaller size needle or hook size.

Blocking and pressing knits and crochet

When you have finished the parts of the crocheted or knitted item, they need to be smoothed out. Check the yarn label for pressing instructions. Then pin out each piece of knitting or crochet (wrong side up) to the required size (called "blocking") and cover it with a damp cloth. If the yarn cannot be pressed, leave the cloth to dry; if it can, lightly press with a warn iron. Then remove the pins.

Weaving in yarn ends

After completing knitted or crocheted pieces, you will have to weave in any loose yarn ends. Thread each yarn end onto a blunt-ended yarn needle, and weave in along the previous row of stitches for a few stitches (or into seams) before snipping off the excess yarn.

Seams on knits and crochet

When stitching pieces of knitted or crocheted fabric together, it is best to do this by hand; use a blunt-ended yarn needle and a single strand of the yarn used for the work.

If you don't want a thick seam on crochet or knitting, place the edges of the two pieces side by side and stitch together by making alternate stitches in each side. Otherwise join fabrics in the usual way, right sides together, with hand backstitches or machine stitching.

Machine topstitching

You can machine topstitch a seam for extra strength or for decoration. To do this, work a row of machine stitches in a matching sewing thread on the right side of the fabric and close to the turned-under edges or seam.

Hand-stitching techniques

You will need to be able to use a needle and thread effectively for most of the projects in this book, and one of them requires some basic hand embroidery, too. In fact, if you can work a few decorative stitches, you can customize some of the projects: for example, add your dog's name to the bag on pages 48–51 or to the roll-up grooming kit holder on pages 34–37.

As some of the stitches in this book employ tapestry wool needlepoint yarn, which is fairly thick, you will need to use a larger-eyed needle than is normally used for embroidery. However, you can choose your own decorative stitching and threads. Thick wool embroidery yarns are suitable for use on fabrics like felt and create a naïve, chunky effect. For a more delicate look, you can split the wool yarn into strands and use a single strand for your stitching.

Backstitch

Backstitch is usually used as a nondecorative stitch to sew fabrics together. Bring the needle and thread through to the right side of the fabric and take a very small stitch backward; bring the needle up again the distance of one small stitch from the last stitch and take another small stitch backward. Repeat to create a row of stitches.

Running stitch

Formed by taking two or three small stitches onto the needle in a sequence and pulling the thread through, running stitch is simple and very quick to work. The picture frame embroidery is worked by making alternating long and short stitches in one row, with a row of short and long stitches in the next row, to form a brick pattern.

Chain stitch

To work chain stitch, you bring the needle up from the wrong side of the fabric and make a loop of thread around the tip of the needle before making a small stitch on the reverse side of the fabric. The following stitches are formed starting inside the tip of the previous stitch, making a chain of stitches, hence the name.

Cross-stitch

Cross-stitches are formed from neat diagonal stitches that cross each other at the center. To create an even row, work them all in the same way, and in the same sequence. Bring needle and thread through from the reverse side of fabric; then make a backward slanting diagonal stitch before bringing the needle up a stitch's distance from into make a crossing diagonal. Repeat for each new stitch.

backstitch

running stitch

chain stitch

cross-stitch

KNITTING AND CROCHET ABBREVIATIONS

The abbreviations used in this book in knitting and crochet are listed below:

Knitting abbreviations

alt	alternate
beg	begin(ning)
cm	centimeter(s)
cont	continu(e)(ing)
dec	decreas(e)(ing)
DK	double-knitting yarn
K	knit
K2tog	knit 2 sts together—one st decreased
foll	follow(ing)
g	gram(s)
m	meter(s)
M1	make 1 stitch; pick up strand between next st and st just worked with tip of left needle, then knit into back of it—one st increased
MC	main color
mm	millimeter(s)
in	inch(es)
inc	increas(e)(ing)
oz	ounce(s)
patt	pattern
P	purl
P2tog	purl 2 sts together—one st decreased
rem	remain(s)(ing)
rep	repeat
RS	right side
skp	slip 1, knit 1, pass slipped st over—one st decreased
st(s)	stitch(es)
St st	stockinette stitch
tog	together
tbl	through back of loop
WS	wrong side
[ ]	Work instructions within brackets as many times as instructed
*	Work instructions following askerisk as directed

Crochet abbreviations

ch	chain(s)
dc	double crochet
yo	yarn over hook

HOW TO CROCHET

Only one basic stitch is used in this book: double crochet. If you have not worked crochet before, it is important that you master the first steps, which includes holding the yarn and hook correctly so that the yarn flows consistently and evenly from the ball, as well as single and half double crochet.

Holding the hook and yarn

You can hold the hook in various ways, but one of the simplest and easiest methods is to hold the hook like you would a pencil, as shown below. If you prefer, you can hold the hook in the palm of your hand, between your thumb and first two fingers, like a knife.

To control an even flow of yarn from the ball of working yarn, thread the yarn through the fingers of the left hand (if you are right-handed) with a single twist around the little finger, and with the yarn then running behind the fourth and third fingers, and over the index finger.

When working crochet, hold the base of the crochet with the first two fingers of the hand holding the yarn. This allows you to create some tension on the yarn, which is essential when pulling the hook and looped yarn through the stitches.

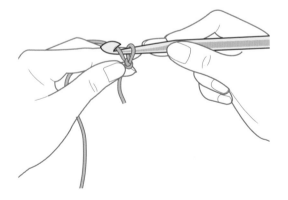

First loop

To start to crochet, you need to create a first loop on the hook. First, form the yarn into a loop, held in place between the thumb and the index finger, and position the ball end of the yarn behind the loop. Then insert the hook through the center of the loop, catch the yarn strand behind the loop with the crochet hook, draw it through, and pull the yarn ends to tighten the first loop around the hook.

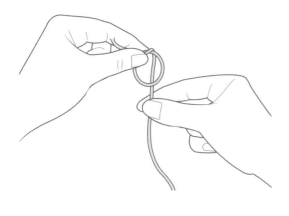

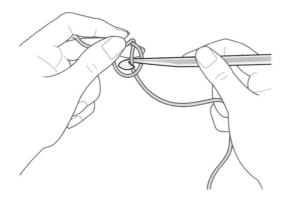

Foundation chain

To make the foundation chain for your crochet, make your first loop, catch the yarn with the hook by passing the hook over and under the yarn in a twisting motion as shown by the arrow, and then draw the yarn through. Continue to make as many chains as required in this way. Take care not to make them too tight.

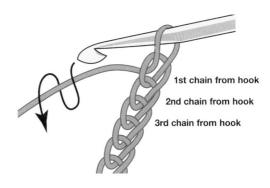

1st chain from hook
2nd chain from hook
3rd chain from hook

Fastening off

To fasten off a piece of crochet when it is complete, first cut the thread about 6in (15cm) from the work. Then pass the loose end through the one remaining loop on the hook, and pull tightly. Weave the loose ends into the wrong side of the work, using a blunt-ended yarn needle.

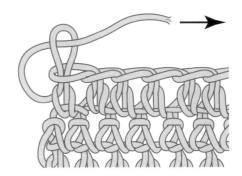

Single crochet

Single crochet is the most commonly used stitch in crochet and is abbreviated in patterns as *sc*. It is also known as "plain stitch" and creates a dense, hard-wearing textile.

1 Make a foundation chain (see page 59); then insert the hook through the SECOND chain from the hook and wrap the yarn around the hook (known as *yarn over hook* or *yo*).

2 Draw the hook through the chain so that there are now two loops on the hook.

3 Wrap the yarn around the hook and draw it through the two loops on the hook—one loop remains on the hook. Work a single crochet in each of the remaining chains in the same way. On the following rows, work the one turning chain (called *chain one* or *ch 1*; see below), then work one single crochet in each stitch of the previous row.

Turning chains

You will need to work a specific number of chains (known as turning chains) at the beginning of a row to bring the hook to the right position for the height of the stitches in the new row.

   When working a pattern, the turning chains count as the first stitch in the row for all simple stitches taller than a single crochet stitch.

Single crochet—ch 1
Half double crochet—ch 2
Double crochet—ch 3

1

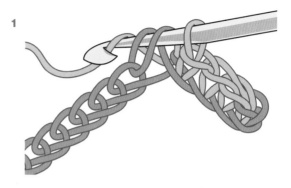

2

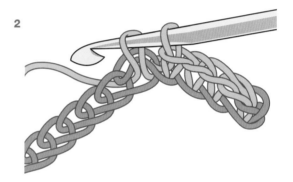

3

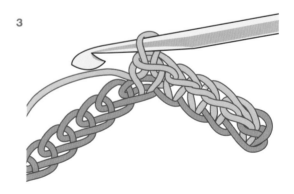

SIMPLE GIFTS FOR DOG LOVERS

Half double crochet

Half double crochet is abbreviated as *hdc* in patterns. It is made in a similar way to single crochet but an additional twist of yarn is made around the hook before the stitch is started. The resulting fabric is slightly more flexible than single crochet.

1 Make a foundation chain; then wrap the yarn around the hook and insert the hook through the THIRD chain from the hook.

2 Wrap the yarn around the hook and draw it through the chain so that there are now three loops on the hook.

3 Wrap the yarn around the hook again and draw it through all three loops on the hook to complete the stitch—one loop remains on the hook. Work a half double crochet in each of the remaining chains in the same way. To start the following rows, first work the two turning chains (to count as the first stitch of the new row). Then skip the first stitch in the previous row and work one stitch in each of the remaining stitches, working the last stitch in the top of the turning chain.

1

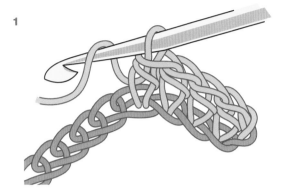

2

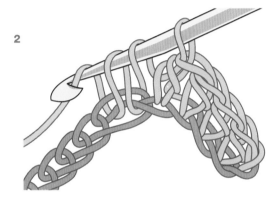

3

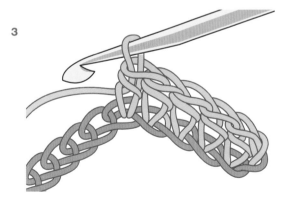

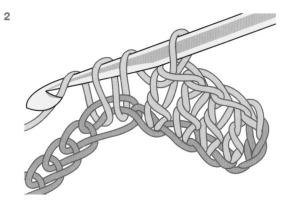

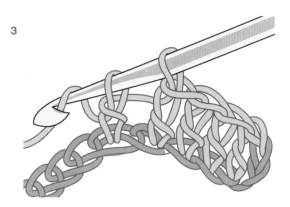

Double crochet

A double crochet stitch is a tall stitch so you can create a supple crochet fabric with it fairly quickly.

1 Make a foundation chain; then wrap the yarn around the hook and insert the hook through the FOURTH chain from the hook.

2 Wrap the yarn around the hook and draw it through the chain so that there are now three loops on the hook. Wrap the yarn around the hook and draw it through the first two loops on the hook.

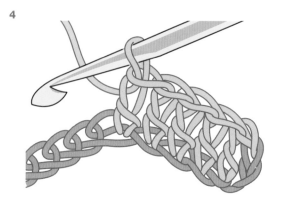

3 There are now two loops on the hook. Wrap the yarn around the hook and draw it through the two remaining loops on the hook.

4 One loop remains on the hook. Work a double crochet in each subsequent chain in the same way. To start the following rows, first work the three turning chains (to count as the first stitch of the new row). Then skip the first stitch in the previous row and work one stitch in each of the remaining stitches, working the last stitch in the top of the turning chain.

BACKINGS AND LININGS

Here are some tips for backing the dog beds and lining the bag in the book.

Bed backings

For the projects that have a removable filling, such as the two dog beds on pages 22–29, you need to create an envelope-shaped backing by attaching the top of the bed to two separate, overlapping pieces of backing fabric. The batting inside the bed can then be inserted and removed when necessary.

1 Make the top of the bed as instructed. Then cut out two pieces of backing fabric to the width of the top and each at least 7¾in (19.5cm) longer than half its length. Fold and press a hem to the wrong side along one short edge of each piece, and stitch it in place.

2 Overlap the two backing pieces and place them wrong side down with the top facing them and wrong side up (see below). Pin and stitch the pieces together around the outer edge; then turn the envelope right side out.

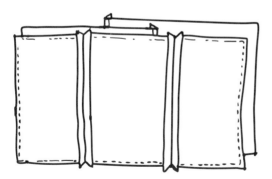

Making a bag lining

Follow these steps to make a fabric lining for the bag on pages 48–51.

1 Cut out two pieces of lining fabric to the same size as one side of the bag, plus ½in (1.5cm) all around the edge for seam allowances. Put these lining pieces to one side while you sew together the two sides of the bag and sew on the bag handles.

2 With the two pieces of lining fabric right sides together, stitch around the two side edges and the bottom edge of the bag. Turn the lining right side out.

3 Slip the lining over the wrong side of the bag, and fold the seam allowance at the top of the lining to the wrong side. Either machine stitch close to the folded edge or slip stitch the lining in place by hand. Turn the bag right side out.

MATERIALS AND YARNS

Choosing a knitting or crochet yarn

To choose a yarn for a knitting or crochet project, first look for a similar yarn weight to the yarn specified in the pattern. Only two yarn weights are used in this book: a double-knitting-weight wool-mix yarn (a "no. 3"-weight following the Craft Yarn Council of America's Yarn Weight System at YarnStandards.com) and an Aran-weight wool-mix yarn (a "no. 4"-weight) as follows—

Double-knitting-weight wool-mix yarn :

55 percent wool, 25 percent acrylic, 20 percent nylon; 1¾oz (50g) and approximately 131yd (120m) per ball; recommended gauge—22 stitches and 30 rows to 4in (10cm) measured over St st using size 6 (4mm) needles.

Aran-weight wool-mix yarn : 70 percent wool,

30 percent alpaca; 1¾oz (50g) and approximately 78yd (74m) per ball; recommended stitch gauge—16.5 stitches and 22 rows to 4in (10cm) measured over St st using size 9 (5.5mm) needles.

Next, try to find a yarn with a similar texture if you want to achieve the same textural effect as the original. Then look at the yarn label to see if the recommended gauge and knitting needle size is close to the specified gauge and needle size in the pattern.

Lastly, be sure to buy the quantity of yarn by the number of yards (meters) required rather than by weight.

Good matches for the double-knitting-weight yarn are: Jaeger *Extra Fine Merino DK*, *Matchmaker DK*, or *Aqua*; or Rowan *Felted Tweed*, *Wool Cotton*, *Tapestry*, or *Scottish Tweed DK*. Good matches for the Aran-weight yarn are: Rowan *Scottish Tweed Aran* or *All Seasons Cotton*.

Felt and fabric

The Coats craft felts used in this book are fully washable and come in small pieces, each measuring approximately 11¾in (30cm) by 9¼in (23.5cm). If the project instructions call for a larger piece of felt, stitch two small pieces together and cut to the correct size.

The other fabrics used in this book are all Rowan printed cottons. They are 100 percent cotton fabrics, fully machine washable, and are approximately 45in (115cm) wide. Any similar cotton patchwork fabrics could be used.

Where to obtain yarns and fabrics

For Rowan or Jaeger yarns, or Rowan fabrics, contact:
Westminster Fibers Inc.
165 Ledge Street
Nashua, New Hampshire 03063
Tel: 1 (800) 445-9276.
E-mail: rowan@westminsterfibers.com
Website: westminsterfibers.com
For tapestry wool needlepoint yarn, use Anchor (as used in this book and available online) or DMC (widely available in craft stores).

ACKNOWLEDGMENTS

The author and publishers would like to thank the following people for their help with this book: Penny Hill for finishing the projects and for pattern writing, John Heseltine for the photographs, Ed Berry for the cover photograph and illustrations, Anne Wilson for the design.

Many thanks also to the dogs and their owners: the Rosa family and Gangster; Ruth and Monty; David, Caroline, and Dennis; and Stuart, Janice, and Duke.

Thanks also to the team at Coats UK for their help and support.